FIGHTING WOLVES

C000154764

FIGHTING WOLVES

God's Amazing Works
in the Days of the Early Church

J.R. WILLIAMSON
R.M. FREEDMAN

CF4·K

10 9 8 7 6 5 4 3 2 1
© Copyright 2013 J.R. Williamson and R.M. Freedman
ISBN: 978-1-78191-154-9

Published by Christian Focus Publications,
Geanies House, Fearn, Tain, Ross-shire,
IV20 1TW, Scotland, U.K.
www.christianfocus.com
E-mail: info@christianfocus.com
Cover design by Daniel van Straaten
Cover illustration by Neil Reed

Character and chapter illustrations by Neil Reed
Illustrations in chapter 2 and 7 by Jeff Anderson
Maps by Neil Reed
Printed and bound by Bell and Bain, Glasgow

This book uses American English spelling.

CONTENTS

LET'S GET STARTED

In the modern world, wolves have become rather popular. They appear on T-shirts looking noble. They get cast in movies as loyal companions. If fairy tales were being written today, instead of being the villain, the wolf would be defending those three little pigs from the farmer who wanted to take them to market, and escorting that little girl in the red hood safely through the woods.

In the past, wolves had pretty nasty reputations, and it's not hard to see why. Back before so many people lived in cities, most of their food and income came from what they could grow, or the farm animals they could raise. If some sneaky four-footed predator started killing their livestock, well, their families would suffer and maybe go hungry.

In a particularly bad year wolves might even attack people.

Nowadays, wolves' behavior is defended because, after all they were just following their instincts. The wolves, it is argued, didn't know that they were causing hardship for the farmers. This is true. Wolves are animals; they go over to the nearest flock, and take what they want – always supposing they can do so without running into an angry shepherd who knows how to drive them away!

The Bible takes this truth about wolves and uses it to illustrate the characteristics of false teachers in the church, men and women who pretend to follow Christ and by their lies attempt to destroy the faith of true Christians and gain power for themselves. Like real wolves, they're cunning predators who care only about what they want, and don't care who may be hurt by what they do.

In the book of Acts, when the Apostle Paul was getting ready to leave the church in Ephesus, he warned the elders that after he had departed "savage wolves will come in among you, not sparing the flock. Also from among yourselves men will rise up, speaking perverse things, to draw away the disciples after themselves" (Acts 20:29 NKJV). He warned them that, like all good shepherds, their duty was to be vigilant, and watch out for these men, and drive them off by proclaiming the truth instead. Not only in Ephesus, but throughout the entire history of the church these wolf-like teachers have attempted to wreak havoc among Christians, and God has always raised up His servants to fight against them.

So come with me back to the very early years of the church, and see God's servants battling the lies of "savage wolves."

JESUS' THREE "MIGHTY MEN"

The Apostle James

If you were asked to name the apostles of the Lord
Jesus, who would be the first ones to come to your
mind? Probably the Apostle Paul would come first.
He is pretty much the main character in one of the
most exciting books in the Bible, the Book of Acts!

Or, perhaps you would think of Peter, the
spokesman for the twelve disciples. He seemed to be
the first to do everything: the first to speak when

Jesus asked a question, the first (in fact, the only one!) to jump out of the boat and walk on water when his Lord told him to, the first to grab a sword and whack away at Jesus' enemies, even when this was exactly the wrong thing to do. Or, if not Paul or Peter, it would probably have to be John, the "disciple whom Jesus loved," the young man who wrote more pages of the New Testament than even Paul, and who lived to be an old man in his Lord's service, dying in exile after receiving a glorious vision of God's ultimate purposes for His people.

Well, you're in good company. If you had asked anyone in Israel this question while Jesus walked

12

the earth, and for a few years after His Resurrection, do you know the first three names they would have said? "Peter, of course, and then James, and, oh yes, his brother John."

In the Old Testament, King David had his "mighty men" who followed him, and out of all these mighty men he had three who were so special they were called *The First Three* (1 Chronicles 11:11–18). That is what Peter, James and John were to the Lord Jesus. Whenever Jesus had something out of the ordinary that he was going to do, whether it was raising the dead to life, or talking to Moses and Elijah, or praying to the Father just before the most momentous act in

the history of the world, He always took with Him these three men who were closest to Him.

Do you remember how they first came to follow Jesus? They had met Him before—Peter's brother, Andrew, who had been a disciple of John the Baptist, had taken Peter to meet the Lord early in His ministry, and since James and John were partners with them in a fishing business, no doubt they came along. But they did not seriously begin to follow Him until one day when Jesus used one of their boats as an informal pulpit. Peter and Andrew, and James and John with their father Zebedee had been trying to catch fish all night without success, and were washing out their empty nets when the Lord Jesus came by. He was being followed by a crowd of people wanting to hear Him teach, so He got into Peter's boat and asked him to cast out a little way onto the lake, and then taught the people from there. This way, He could easily be seen and heard without the people crowding all around Him, and they could stand or sit on the shore and just listen. When he had finished teaching, He told Peter to "Launch out into the deep and let down your nets for a catch" (Luke 5:4-6 NKJV). Peter didn't think this was a very good idea—and he was careful to let the Lord know it! He said, "Master, we have toiled all night and caught nothing; nevertheless at Your word I will let down the net." However, when he obeyed, so many fish filled the net that it began to break, and he had to yell for James and John to come quickly in the other boat to help. When they got there, they filled both boats with so many fish that they began to sink under the weight! They were still wondering and exclaiming about where all these fish had come from – when the Lord said to them, "Follow Me, and I will make you fishers of men." They didn't hesitate. The Bible says that they brought their boats to the shore, and immediately left their nets (and that enormous catch of fish) with the others, and "forsook all and followed Him" (Luke 5:1-11 NKJV).

These men were the first ones the Lord Jesus chose to be His disciples, and when the twelve apostles are listed, they are always mentioned first. You may remember that Peter's name was actually Simon, but that Jesus gave him the nickname of "Cephas"— meaning a stone, or a rock (Peter is the Greek form of this word). He called him this, not because Simon was built like a boulder, or because he was particularly stable when the Lord first chose him, but because the Lord meant to transform his character into someone who would be a source of rock-like strength to the young and struggling church. James and John, however, apparently got their nicknames not because of who they would be one day, but because of how they were then: Jesus called them "Boanerges" which means "Sons of Thunder" (Mark 3:17). What do you think of when you think of thunder? Is it a polite and timid noise, like someone knocking on a door asking to come in? No, it's loud and aggressive, and immediately catches your attention. If it's close enough, it even makes you jump; you probably want to look for the nearest shelter, because you know dangerous lightning might not be far behind! Apparently, this is what those two young fishermen were like, bold and with a kind of take-no-prisoners attitude.

For three years, Peter and James and John were Jesus's closest companions. He took them to places where none of the other disciples were permitted to go. When Jairus, the ruler of the synagogue, came and begged Jesus to heal his little daughter, "He permitted no one to follow Him except Peter, James, and John the brother of James" (Mark 5:37 NKJV). And when they arrived at the house and found the little girl already dead, Jesus ran everyone out of the room except her parents and His three disciples, who were allowed to stay and witness His power over death. "Then he took the child by the hand, and said to her, 'Talitha, Cumi,' which is translated, 'Little girl, I say to you, arise.' Immediately the girl arose and walked, for she was twelve years of age. And they were overcome with great amazement. But he commanded them strictly that no one should know it, and said that something should be given her to eat" (Mark 5:37–43 NKJV).

Later in His ministry He chose them to be the ones who would not "taste death till they see the kingdom of God present with power" (Mark 9:1 NKJV). He took them "up on a high mountain apart by themselves; and he was transfigured before them. His clothes became shining, exceedingly white, like snow, such as no launderer on earth can whiten them" (Mark 9:2-3 NKJV). This was but the slightest glimpse of His true glory, which he had concealed by taking on our humanity to save us. The three friends were still blinking in astonishment at the sight when they realized that those two strange men he was talking to were Moses and Elijah! Peter was so overcome that he thought the best thing to do would be for them to set up sturdy shelters, so they could all stay up there longer! But then something even more astounding happened, for suddenly they found themselves overshadowed by a bright cloud, and "a voice came out of the cloud saying, 'This is my beloved Son, in whom I am well pleased. Hear Him.'" The three disciples were terrified, and fell on their faces, too afraid even to look up until Jesus "came and touched them and said, 'Arise, and do not be afraid.' When they had lifted up their eyes, they saw no one but Jesus only" (Matthew 17:5-8 NKJV).

As he led them back down the mountain, he commanded "that they should tell no one the things they had seen till the Son of Man had risen from the dead" (Mark 9:9 NKJV). They didn't understand what he meant about "rising from the dead", and apparently didn't dare ask Him at the time. However, they did pluck up enough courage to ask Him why the scribes had always taught that Elijah must come before the Messiah. Clearly, Jesus was the Messiah, and yet they had just now seen Elijah for the first time. Jesus answered and said to them, "Indeed, Elijah is coming first and will restore all things. But I say to you that Elijah has come already, and they did not know him but did to him whatever they wished. Likewise the Son of Man is also about to suffer at their hands." Then the disciples understood that He spoke to them of John the Baptist (Matthew 17: 11-13 NKJV).

Just as they had promised, the three didn't say a word about what they had seen up on that mountain to the other disciples, but you can bet they didn't forget it for a minute. They'd seen Moses, the great law-giver who had talked to God face to face on Mt. Sinai, and Elijah, who had confronted wicked kings and queens and called down fire from heaven to humiliate the false priests of Baal. Not only that, but they'd seen their Master, their kind and patient Rabbi, shining like the sun, and being treated by these holy men with reverence! Surely, Israel's long-awaited Messiah was here and about to reveal His power to everyone, and take vengeance on all of God's enemies! What an exciting time to live in—and these three fishermen, James and John, sons of Zebedee, and their good friend Peter, were privileged to be right in the midst of God's great kingdom work, and among the closest companions to the Messiah Himself!

Now, these three did not necessarily seem like "mighty men." But God was training and preparing them each to stand for Him in the days to come. These days with Jesus while He was on earth strengthened them to face any and every challenge to their faith, and to stand bold and firm for the truth. The history of the church after what is recorded in Acts tells us that each of these men died a courageous death. James was the first to die while risking his life in spreading the gospel (Acts 12:2). Peter is said to have been crucified upside down by the Romans, because he didn't feel worthy to be crucified in the same way as Jesus. And John, though he lived long, suffered banishment and exile on Patmos "on account of the word of God and the testimony of Jesus" (Revelation 1:9 ESV). Because he lived long, he was able to encourage and strengthen a new generation of disciples. So, we see that the line of bold witnesses for the Savior can be traced back to these mighty men and the other disciples from Jesus' time on earth. They set the pattern of holding fast to God's Word, even in the face of severe opposition and the threat of personal harm or even death. As those who saw Jesus in His glory, and had close fellowship with Him, they lived and preached in such a way that people were amazed. Acts tells us: "Now when they saw the boldness of Peter and John ... they were astonished. And they recognized that they had been with Jesus" (Acts 4:13 ESV). And through the centuries that followed, the saints of God have continued to bravely face those who attack and persecute them. If you faithfully walk with Jesus, however weak you may feel yourself, or seem to others, you too will be made brave and bold when persecutions come. The Lord God will always be present with you when the enemies roar, and He will always be faithful to strengthen you to face the lions!

A FAITHFUL FRIEND
Basil the Great (AD 329–379)

Going off to school can make you feel scared and anxious, excited and thankful, or both. In the case of Basil the Great, it was both. (Of course, in his school days, he was just plain old Basil!)

Basil was born a few years after the Council of Nicaea gave their great statement of faith. He is often known as Basil of Caesarea, since that is where he was born, and also spent most of his life. Caesarea was the capital of Cappadocia, in Asia Minor (where Turkey is today).

Basil was one of ten children born into a wealthy Christian family, and though several of his ancestors had in the past been persecuted to the point of death for their faith, by the time Basil was born the emperor Constantine had already made open Christianity much safer, even in the east. As a matter of fact, both Basil and his very good friend Gregory Nazanzien, who also became a well-known Christian leader, went to school together in Basil's hometown. Later, they continued their education to meet again in college at another famous school in the ancient Greek city of Athens. Their college was

known as one of the best in the world at the time. A classmate, during Basil's studies there, would later become one of the most awful emperors the Christians ever had to face. His name was Julian. Just as Basil would later be given the title "the Great" for his works for Christ and the church, Julian also would later be given a title: Julian the Apostate! Apostate means a person who turns away from the Christian faith, and Julian did that in a big way. Even though persecutions had officially ended by this time, he started persecuting believers all over again, and set up many idols throughout the empire. He tried to establish the pagan worship of false gods as the emperors of the past had done.

If you have some mean kids or bullies in your school, then just know that Christian young people have had to face those kinds of pressures for years – going back all the way to ancient times. Just think what it must have been like to have this future dictator as your classmate! Thankfully, Julian's terrorizing ways were cut short by God's hand of judgment. He died in battle at thirty-two years of age, and his last words are some of the most well known among unbelievers. He looked up to heaven and said, as if speaking to Jesus, "You have conquered, Galilean!"

Not only were there such unsavoury characters like Julian in Basil's school, but Athens was a city full of all kinds of distractions and sinful behavior to tempt young men away from their studies. It is a great testimony to Basil's commitment to the Lord that he refused to get into the partying life that other students participated in. A big help to him was his friend Gregory. That friendship helped them to keep each other accountable. Gregory said that his friend Basil had a strong influence for good among all those that knew him. He wrote that there was one main competition between them: "not who was first but who allowed the other to be first. It seemed as if we had one soul in two bodies." God used this friendship for both of them to grow in the grace and knowledge of Jesus Christ. Athens had many streets: streets filled with taverns, streets filled with theaters, and more. So Basil and Gregory agreed together that the only two streets they would know would be two: the street that went from their room to the school, and the street that went to the church!

These two friends wanted to pursue their education, but they wanted to remain dedicated to God and lead holy lives even more than to "graduate with honors." Basil taught afterward that though classical studies were not bad in themselves, he thought they should always be pursued warily, and with one's gaze fixed firmly on the great Christian purpose of eternal life, to which "all earthly objects and attainments are as shadows and dreams to reality." He saw that just because something was considered classic literature, or just because it was taught by an expert, it didn't mean that it was true. The Christian student needed to test all things by the truth God revealed. And he also needed to place value on what promoted the glory of God, not what puffed up man. So, Basil faced the challenge of secular teaching at university, and held more firmly to God's Word in the end.

After Basil completed his studies he returned home to Caesarea, but shortly thereafter he decided to visit the Middle East, going to places like Egypt and Palestine, where he learned about the new movement called monasticism. This was when people lived a very simple, basic life emphasizing prayer and study and time alone for meditation.

By the time he returned home, Basil had decided this was the life for him. He sold his many possessions and from that time forward lived on a sparse diet of not much more than bread and water. He moved to a lonely but beautiful area in Pontus, not far from where his mother and sister lived. Basil loved it there. He wrote his friend Gregory, telling him about the beautiful and peaceful place, and soon Gregory came to live there too. Together they pursued lives of prayer, Scriptural studies, and useful labor, surrounded by waterfalls, singing birds, blooming plants, and flourishing wildlife. Here, separated from the distractions of worldly things, Basil was confident that he could serve God best. He thought that "silent solitude is the beginning of purification of the soul."

Unfortunately, as other godly men could have told him, attempting to fix his mind on heavenly things by physically withdrawing from worldly affairs doesn't always work. Basil was eventually forced to admit that he had failed to leave behind one particular source of trouble: himself. "I have well forsaken my residence in the city as a source of a thousand evils," he lamented at one point to a friend, "but I have not been able to forsake myself."

However, as a true servant of God, Basil was not content just to devote himself to peaceful studies and a contemplation of nature. As always, the church was beset by false teachers from within and less-subtle enemies from without, and Basil soon found himself busy defending the truth. False teachers were still trying to claim that Jesus was not truly God. So Basil wrote five books defending the deity of Christ. When believers saw how well Basil understood and taught the Scriptures, they came to him in his peaceful retreat and took him to Caesarea to pastor the church there. So much for his life of peaceful solitude!

Though he was now in the thick of things, Basil kept his simple lifestyle. He still ate only bread and water for the most part, and had few earthly possessions. But if he didn't take very good care of his own body, he was very compassionate toward others, and was always ready to care for the poor and sick. The lepers in the region especially drew his attention. Most people were so horrified by this disease that they would cast out their own family members who had it, forcing them to live or die on the streets as best they could. Basil worked hard to have a hospital built chiefly for these outcast sufferers, and knowing how everyone else feared to come near them, he would make it a point to accept them into the hospital himself. Basil would greet them and touch them kindly, instead of drawing away in disgust. This hospital became famous, and was called the Basilias. Like his Savior before him, Basil's heart was drawn to those that society had cast off. Basil ministered not only to lepers and the poor, but even thieves and prostitutes. Where he saw physical or moral need, he encouraged believers to show forth the love of Christ.

A few years after Basil was first ordained, his preaching and his service to the people brought about his election as the bishop of Caesarea and the surrounding areas. This meant he was responsible to oversee more than fifty churches. He began to seek to restore health to these churches and make sure they understood and believed the truth about Christ. He wrote many letters to the pastors of these churches, urging them not to live a comfortable life of ease, but to give generously and work tirelessly. As someone who himself had sold his family inheritance to give to the needy, Basil certainly practiced what he preached.

His work gained the attention of the ruler of the eastern part of the Roman Empire, Emperor Valens. The emperor was trying to lead all the churches in the opposite direction, promoting a low view of Christ that made him little more than a great created angel, rather than the Lord of Glory. So, he saw Basil as a threat. Valens recognized Basil as the one standing in the way of his desire to impose Arianism on all the churches in the East, and he had Basil threatened with confiscation, banishment, and death. Basil was not impressed, and said, "Nothing more? Not one of these things touches me." He pointed out that he had nothing that could be confiscated, since he no longer owned any property; he couldn't be banished because he was only a guest of God, who owned the whole earth; and death would only be a kindness, because it would send him more quickly to God.

Nevertheless, Valens was determined to at least banish him from Caesarea, but just as he was about to do so, Valens' little son became sick, and all the doctors said he was dying. The emperor sent for Basil as a last resort, asking him to pray for the prince, and after Basil had prayed the boy did recover, though only for a little while. At about the same time one of the emperor's officials, who had been harsh and unpleasant to Basil, recovered from a serious illness. Basil had prayed for him as well, and together the two incidents diffused the emperor's desire to banish the bishop. It seemed that God was with Basil, so maybe it wasn't such a good idea to send him too far away!

Basil's life as a bishop was never easy. He continued to struggle against divisions and hostility from enemies of God for the rest of his life. He fought against them with his pen and prayers and sermons. No doubt he thought longingly of the quiet life he had left behind in his beautiful valley, before reminding himself that God placed his faithful servants where He needed them.

However, Basil did not really have many years to wait before he left the turmoil and troubles of this world behind, and went to the place of eternal rest, the right hand of God, where there are pleasures forevermore (Psalm 16:11). Continually afflicted by spiritual and mental trials as he sought to protect his flock and preserve peace and unity within the church, and nourished only by his sparse diet, his body wasted away around his fiftieth year. He passed into God's presence quoting the Scripture: "Into thy hands, O Lord I commit my spirit; you have redeemed me, O Lord, God of truth." Multitudes of Christians joined the funeral procession, knowing that their beloved bishop had passed into eternal life, but that they had lost a good and faithful shepherd for their souls.

DEVOTIONAL THOUGHT

We read in the life of Basil, how helpful and influential his friendship with Gregory was. They helped each other stay out of trouble in school, and challenged one another to great devotion to the Lord. It reminds us of the relationship between David and Jonathan. When David was hiding from Saul and fearing for his life, Jonathan came and "strengthened his hand in God" (1 Samuel 23:16 NKJV). He risked the anger of his father to go and comfort his friend when he needed it. He helped David remember that the Lord had promised to be with him and to make him king. He reminded him of God's truth, which David really needed to hear at that moment.

Christian friends are indeed a gift from God, and I urge you to pray for and seek out friends like that – friends that will keep your eyes on Jesus. None of us can make it through all the dangers in this world on our own. We need the help and accountability of others in the church. We need to spend time with those whose warmth for the Lord warms us up as well. You and I need people that will be there for us as we face life's trials. If you don't see any prospects for a friend like that right now, start praying! The Lord will send along a true friend in time, who can be a Jonathan to you, and you to them.

NO ONE ABOVE GOD'S LAW:

Ambrose of Milan (AD 340-397)

When the emperor Constantine declared Christianity the official religion of the Roman Empire, he probably had no idea that this would mean that one day an emperor would be made to humble himself before a bishop, but that is what happened with Bishop Ambrose of Milan and the emperor Theodosius.

Of course, when Ambrose was merely a governor in northern Italy he never would have thought of commanding the emperor, either, for at that time it was his duty to submit to those in authority over him. But when, in God's plan, Ambrose was made a bishop, his duties changed, as we shall see.

Ambrose was born in Germany (which was part of the Empire), but educated in Rome, learning literature and law, and how to speak in public. His parents were Christians, but now that Constantine had made that respectable, his father was also a high-ranking government official, and Ambrose followed in his footsteps, apparently going about his duties so faithfully and with such fairness that he got a very good reputation throughout the city.

During this time the controversy between the Arians and those who held to the Nicene Creed continued to drag on, encouraged by various emperors, who favored first one side and then another. There were some bishops who believed one thing and some another. The bishops were pastors of local churches, but in bigger cities, this meant they would lead and preach to a lot of people. As well, in some of the largest cities, the bishops also advised and helped support other churches. Later on, bishops became less involved in one particular church, but that was not yet the case in the days of Ambrose.

While Ambrose was still a young man one of the Arian bishops died, and there was a big uproar about who would take his place, since both sides were determined to get "their man" in place. Well, Ambrose was a good churchman, so of course he was interested in the outcome of the election. He went to the church where it was going on, hoping to be able to calm the people down a bit, as everyone was afraid a riot would be started by whichever side lost. He was apparently known for his charitableness toward the Arians, even though he didn't agree with them, and so while he was speaking someone cried out, "Ambrose, bishop!" even though his name wasn't on the ballot. Soon everyone was shouting for him to be the next bishop, and completely ignoring the other men who had been considered for the office. Ambrose

tried to tell them he wasn't prepared for such a role—he wasn't even baptized! (Some people thought you should wait until you were dying to be baptized.) But no matter how much he protested, the people didn't listen. They appointed him bishop anyway, so he went to hide out with a friend: maybe he thought that when they couldn't find him they'd lose interest in appointing him! But then his friend received a letter from the emperor himself, supporting the decision to make Ambrose a bishop, and so his friend promptly snitched on him. At this point Ambrose apparently gave up protesting, and he was baptized and became Bishop of Milan, in Italy. This made everybody happy and comfortable with the choice—except Ambrose!

Unfortunately for the Arians, it seems that while Ambrose was perfectly willing to be charitable toward those who disagreed with his faith when he was just a common member of a congregation, once he was put in a position of authority, he took his new sacred responsibilities as seriously as he had taken his government work. First of all, he sold just about everything he had in order to give to the poor. Then, he had to read up on his theology! Although the Arians might be nice enough people and sincere in their beliefs, their beliefs were still wrong and God's punishment for this unbelief was hell. As a bishop, Ambrose could not tolerate this false teaching. He began to speak out against the heresy, and put a stop to it wherever he could. You can imagine the Arians' shock and dismay, since they had helped to make him bishop. They couldn't even complain that he had lied in order to get their vote, since he had never wanted to be elected in the first place!

The emperor was also in for a big surprise. Being the ruler of the Roman Empire, he was pretty much used to doing anything his power and his armies would let him do. Even though he was called a Christian, since that was the official religion all emperors were supposed to be, Theodosius had some questionable practices. He saw to it that some government money went to pagan temples and statues and things like that, and he had an uncontrolled temper as well. But once the emperor was in Ambrose's church, he soon learned that it was not enough to just say you were a Christian.

In AD 390, the emperor came up against Bishop Ambrose's conscience, and it was a mighty collision! Theodosius had gotten angry with the city of Thessalonica because some rioters there had murdered its governor. To punish them, since it was impossible to track down the actual rioters, he sent his army in and had 7,000 Thessalonians killed. This explosion of his temper didn't seem to bother him, though many innocent people had died because of it. He does not seem to have given a thought to God's displeasure with him over these murders—until he was excommunicated from the church under the leadership of Ambrose. This still did not phase the emperor, and he tried to show up at church as usual the next Lord's Day. Ambrose refused to allow him to enter. The emperor said, "But I've repented." However, his pastor replied that his repentance should be as public as his sin had been. Unless he demonstrated his remorse for everyone to see, he could not be received back into the church! Such a serious sin required signs of true heartfelt grief and a new direction of life. He told Theodosius that King David of Israel had not been able to get away with murder, even though he was a man "after God's own heart," and that if the emperor was going to act like David in the matter of guilt (though King David only had one man unlawfully killed, not thousands), then he must repent like David as well.

I expect that when Theodosius received this message his jaw dropped; then he was probably furious, and made sure everyone around him knew it. Ambrose, however, knew God's Law, and he knew his duty. No man, no matter how powerful, is above it; we are all equal in God's eyes in this respect. The church was not open to those who lived in unrepentant sin, even if they ruled the largest empire in the world! Furthermore, Ambrose said that if he let Theodosius go on in his sin without warning him, God would hold him, Ambrose, responsible for the emperor's destruction, as it says in Ezekiel 3:18. This was an important conflict, because the church was learning to deal with emperors who claimed to be Christians: a new thing from the earlier days of persecution. Was the church to submit to the emperor, or the emperor submit to the church? Over time, it would become clear that both should happen. The church has responsibilities to the government (Romans 13), but it cannot let the government tell it what to teach, how to worship God, or who should be in or out of the church (Acts 5:29; Ephesians 1:22-23). It is Christ and Christ alone who is head of the church, and that was the issue when Ambrose and Theodosius faced one another regarding Theodosius' sin.

This "face off" ended eight months later, when the emperor returned to the church, publicly expressing his true sorrow over his sin, weeping and asking to be restored. Then, he was returned to the fellowship of his church. After this, he no longer gave any support to pagan customs and religions, but instead issued decrees designed to discourage paganism entirely. Also, Theodosius held to the Nicene Creed from then on.

Later, Theodosius would say about Ambrose that he was the only real bishop that the emperor had ever known. The boldness and lack of partiality in Ambrose was great to see. However, like all of us, he had shortcomings. Sometimes Ambrose overstretched his authority in counseling—almost ordering—the emperor to take certain actions for Christians. These actions often went beyond justice into favoritism. In future generations, some church leaders took this precedent and abused government power in the church. But with Ambrose, his main concern was to keep the church from cowering before any earthly ruler, or changing its teaching and practice because of riches and power.

You might think from what you have learned about Ambrose so far that he did nothing but fight against the enemies of orthodoxy and confront erring sovereigns, but in fact Ambrose believed that a pastor's first duty was to be a preacher of the Word of God, and he became famous for his sermons. Unlike many preachers, he wanted to keep his teaching centered on what the Bible said, and would take passages from the Old Testament and build his sermons around them. Though some of his methods of interpreting were unusual, he got the main thing right, as he faithfully and eloquently preached the gospel week by week.

Ambrose eventually became "known throughout the world," for his sermons and his devotion to God. In fact, his speaking ability was so much admired that unconverted people would sometimes come to hear him preach even when they had no interest in Christianity! One of these was named Augustine, and even though at first he cared nothing for what Ambrose was preaching about, when he met him he found the bishop so kind that his heart began to change toward Christianity. Eventually Ambrose had the happiness of baptizing this young man who had originally only come to hear a good speaker.

Although it might seem that helping to defeat Arianism and bringing an emperor to his knees was sufficient to establish Ambrose's importance in church history, it was through this man Augustine's conversion, and the vast impact his writings were going to have on the entire Western world, that Ambrose made perhaps his greatest contribution to the church.

Ambrose was not that old when he fell very sick. His friends were all praying for his recovery, and they urged him to do so as well, but he replied, "I have not lived among you in such a way, that I would have to be ashamed to live longer; but I am also not afraid of death, for we have a good Lord." Soon after this, Ambrose laid aside the title of bishop which he had so reluctantly accepted, and joyfully went to meet his "good Lord" face to face.

DEVOTIONAL THOUGHT

People in power are given their power by the all powerful God. They are not above God. God is in control of all that he has made and it is because of God's power and his will that men and women have any influence over God's creation. Sometimes God blesses us with wise and perhaps even godly leadership. He certainly has in the past. However, today our leaders are often not Christians. Does that mean we don't have to obey them? No. We are responsible to submit to the authority of the government as part of the structure of society God has made. Here is what the Bible says: It is necessary to submit to the authorities, not only because of possible punishment but also as a matter of conscience. This is also why you pay taxes, for the authorities are God's servants, who give their full time to governing. Give to everyone what you owe them:

> "If you owe taxes, pay taxes; if revenue, then revenue; if respect, then respect; if honor, then honor" (Romans 13:7 NIV)

Ambrose and Theodosius lived at a time when power changed hands frequently. Both the church and the state had to recognise the power of each other. We all have to recognise that power is God given; it ultimately all belongs to him. Nothing is outside of his control.

FACT FILE

There is a rather unusual story involving Ambrose and bees. It was said that as an infant, a swarm of bees settled on his face while he lay in his cradle, leaving behind a drop of honey. His father declared that it was this drop of honey that gave his son a honeyed tongue. For this reason, bees and beehives often appear in pictures and stories about Ambrose.

THE GOLDEN MOUTH COULD NOT BE SILENCED:

Chrysostom (AD 346-407)

I said before that the name "John" is scattered throughout church history. This next man of God was actually named John, but is always known in church history as Chrysostom [KRIS-ah-stum], even though that is just a nickname meaning "golden mouthed," which was given to him because he was such a good speaker.

John "Chrysostom" was born in Antioch about the same time as Ambrose was born in Italy, and there are several similarities in their lives. For instance, they were both well educated for a life of secular employment, they were both appointed to a high church office against their wills, and they both confronted emperors! The big difference is, that in the Western part of the Roman Empire, where Ambrose was, the church's authority had come to be stronger even than that of the secular state, while in the Eastern part it had remained much weaker. This difference is clearly displayed in what happened to each man: both were faithful men of God, and yet one saw an emperor bow in humility at his insistence, while the other saw himself banished from the city he loved.

We know very little about Chrysostom's family. His father was an officer in the army, but as he died when Chrysostom was just a baby it was left to his mother to raise him and see to his education. We don't even know if she was a Christian or not, but it seems likely that she was, since even though she decided to send him to a well-known pagan teacher for his schooling, Chrysostom was also baptized when he was a very young man. Despite excelling in his studies under his pagan teacher, Chrysostom became increasingly uninterested in the public career planned for him, and more and more drawn to the things of God. When he finally abandoned his pagan teacher to go study Christian theology, it is said that the man was very disappointed—he had thought so highly of Chrysostom that he had been planning to let him take over the school eventually, but "the Christians took him away from us." This is surely a good testimony of Chrysostom's life.

Chrysostom seems to have been one of those people who throw themselves enthusiastically into whatever they are doing from a spiritual motivation. He is a good illustration of Colossians 3:23 NKJV, "Whatever you do, do it heartily, as to the Lord." He left Antioch to live in a distant monastery, where apparently he took up a life of great simplicity and self-denial, to the point that he was so busy memorizing the Bible, he hardly allowed himself time to sit down and rest or go to sleep, and he barely ate and drank enough to keep himself alive. Not surprisingly, his health gave out and he had to return to more moderate ways of living. However, for the rest of his life he had to deal with the damage he had caused to his body as a zealous young man!

After he returned to Antioch he became first a deacon in the church, and then a priest. You remember his nickname—well, this is the time when he would have earned it. He preached with great eloquence on various books of the Bible, and urged people to care for the poor, and not to let their wealth harden their hearts. One of his sermons pointed out that

Christians were part of the body of Christ whether they were clothed in silk, or freezing to death in rags, and he condemned people who gave expensive gifts to the church instead of using the money to help their poorer brethren who didn't have enough to eat. He had a good rhetorical education and could have used his training to be clever and flowery in his speech and leave everyone talking about how brilliant he was, but instead he chose to teach simply so that people could actually receive help from his sermons. He was willing to take God's word at face value, instead of finding allegories in every passage, and his listeners

were the better for it. He told them how God wanted them to live, but showed them too, setting them an example of charitable work. Later on he even set up several hospitals to care for the poor.

Chrysostom was not afraid to point out sins wherever he saw them, whether it was neglect of the poor or failure to respect governing authorities. One time a number of people were angry at the emperor and so they ran around the city damaging all the statues of him and his family. Everyone knew that the emperor, Theodosius (yes, the same Theodosius

who massacred 7,000 Thessalonians) would punish the city somehow. It grieved Chrysostom that his people participated in these out of control riots, and he began to preach a series of sermons—twenty-one in all—calling the people to repent of wickedness. Antioch was still a city with a great many pagans in it, and these sermons were so powerful and used by God that many of them became Christians, and those who were not converted were affected by his preaching. It is thought that as a result of this vast change of heart among the people, Theodosius decided not to punish them as harshly as he had originally intended.

When he was almost fifty years old, Chrysostom was chosen to be the new Archbishop of Constantinople. Like Ambrose, he didn't think he should have the position, and he didn't want it! In fact, it is said that they had to send a group of soldiers to round him up and hustle him out of Antioch. This was because they were afraid his congregation would make a ruckus about it, and because they suspected he might refuse to come unless he was given no choice. Apparently, by the time he reached Constantinople he was resigned to accepting the position, but that didn't mean that he was going to fall in with what everyone wanted. In fact, he began upsetting people almost at once, because he wouldn't throw lavish parties for all the wealthy and important people like the other archbishops had done. Also, a lot of bad practices had crept into the church, and he started putting a stop to those which really annoyed the other church officials. They had become comfortable with the way things were done. Some priests had begun to leave their small congregations and come to the "big city" in search of more money, and Chrysostom promptly sent them back to where they belonged to serve the people rather than their own purses.

He was just as fearless in confronting secular problems as spiritual ones. His attitude seems to have been that since they had forced him to come to Constantinople and be an archbishop, then he was going to make them all regret it by being the best archbishop he could possibly be.

Theodosius had died and his son Arcadius was emperor in the East. Arcadius had a wife named Aelia Eudoxia, who pretty much ruled over her husband and got him to do whatever she wanted. She was also very fashionable, and liked to dress at great expense. When Chrysostom began preaching against this very thing (Christian women dressing extravagantly instead of modestly), she took it personally—and maybe he meant her to! In any event, she became his enemy, and since he was busy stepping on sensitive, sinful toes all over the place, it wasn't long before his enemies began to plot how to get rid of him.

One of Chrysostom's biggest enemies was a man named Theophilus, who was a high church official in Alexandria. Theophilus had taken a dislike to the doctrines of certain Egyptian monks, so he had sent soldiers after them who burned their homes and treated them badly. When the monks fled to Constantinople and asked Chrysostom for help (which he gave them) it made Theophilus very angry. He had tried several times to make trouble for Chrysostom since then, but after speaking with the empress and others, he came up with a new plan. The emperor had actually summoned him to come to Constantinople alone to answer for his crimes against the Egyptian monks, but instead Theophilus showed up with a bunch of his friends and allies, and together they drew up a whole list of false accusations against Chrysostom and tried to get him to come to the Synod and apologize!

Chrysostom refused to come to such an openly unfair gathering, composed of all his worst enemies, and sadly, the emperor was such a weak man that instead of being outraged at Theophilus's arrogance, he turned against his archbishop and fired him. Chrysostom went quietly when the soldiers came to fetch him, but he was only held for a few days. The people who loved and respected him had raised a commotion about his arrest. Then, an earthquake happened in the city, and the guilty conscience of

Eudoxia made her feel that maybe God was judging them for treating him this way. So she told her husband that Chrysostom must be reinstated. When he returned, joyfully welcomed back by the people, Theophilus and his friends all fled for their lives.

Sadly, the Empress Eudoxia's small bout of repentance didn't last. The vain woman had a silver statue of herself put up near Chrysostom's church, and what went on at the dedication offended him so much that he publicly compared her to wicked Herodias in the Bible, who had brought about the death of John the Baptist. Well, Eudoxia didn't ask for Chrysostom's head, but she threatened to banish him. Chrysostom sent a brave reply back to the empress. He told the messengers from Eudoxia, "Tell her I fear nothing but sin!" So Eudoxia had her husband send him away. For a time, Chrysostom continued to try to minister to his people by writing letters and sending them back to the city. However, annoyed by the fact that he still had such influence even though he was exiled, his enemies saw to it that he was sent further away. But this time his health, broken by his early years of extreme self-denial, gave out altogether and he died on the road to a distant place called Pitiunt, where he was buried. It is said that his last words were, "Glory be to God for all things!"

So, Chrysostom not only had a "golden mouth" but an iron will. Like Ambrose, not even the most powerful ruler could intimidate him. But unlike Ambrose, the ruler in this case chose to punish the preacher rather than repent of the sin. It is good for us to see the contrast between these two men, and remember that our calling to faithfulness is the same, however others respond to the Word of God.

DEVOTIONAL THOUGHT

Chrysostom is described as "fearless." He stood up to evil practices and injustice by church and state.

We mentioned before that he compared the empress to Herodias in the Bible. Well, she was indeed like that wicked ruler's wife. And she used her power a lot like Herodias used hers. In both cases, the ruler himself tolerated the rebuke, but the wife demanded punishment for the preacher. And Chrysostom responded with the same boldness that his namesake John the Baptist did centuries earlier.

How do you think you would have responded? It is certainly scary when those in authority put pressure on us to take back something we say about God's truth. We want to avoid the embarrassment or even punishment that may come. But it is amazing how the Lord comes and ministers peace to our soul when we ask for His help. We are reminded that our "help comes from the Lord, the maker of heaven and earth" (Psalm 121:2 NIV). Like John the Baptist in prison, the Lord sends us a word of encouragement that His work is continuing on, and there is no need to fear (Matthew 11:1-6). Our work is not in vain because it is the Lord's work. And whatever happens to us individually, the spread of the good news about His Son cannot be stopped.

FACT FILE

Alexandria was Egypt's capital until the Muslim conquest of Egypt in AD 641. Ancient Alexandria was best known for its lighthouse and its library (the largest in the ancient world). From the late 19th Century, Alexandria became a major international shipping centre due to its overland access to the Mediterranean Sea and the Red Sea, and its trade in Egyptian cotton.

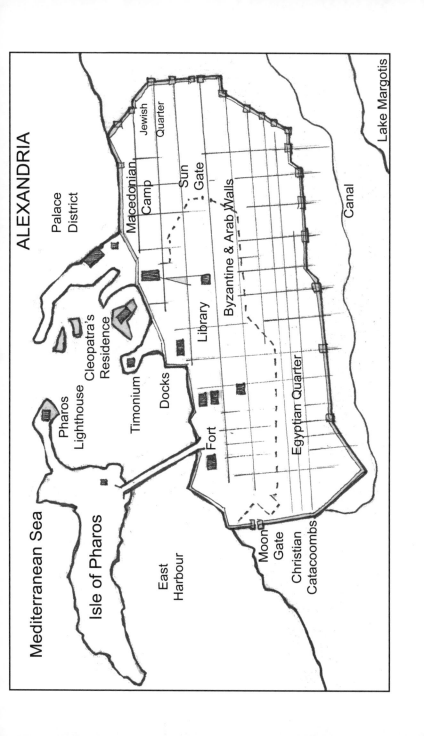

Up, Up, and Away:
Simeon Stylites (AD 390-459)

Some Christians like Anthony[1] tried to get away from people in order to meditate more and give more of their life to Christ. Anthony did this by going further and further into the desert. Other Christians decided to try and do one better. They thought that what was needed was to go up—up into the sky, that is, to sit on top of a pillar! They had huge tall pillars built, with small platforms on top, and then

---
[1] See *Facing Lions* in Risktakers series Chapter 7.

they would go and live on top of the pillars, exposed to all sorts of weather, and totally undistracted by normal life "down there" in the world. Later on, these folks became known as the "Pillar Cult" since they were a strange group with some off-the-wall views of what it means to serve God. But others call them "Pillar Saints" because they were thought to be extra holy people.

However, as it is with any practice like this you must read God's Word to determine whether or not it is in keeping with God's will. For example, if Christians were doing things like this in order to be forgiven by God, or to get to heaven then that was wrong. But some may have built these pillars for other reasons such as self-discipline and meditation. This idea still may seem weird to us though.

The most famous of these "Pillar Saints" was called Simeon Stylites, and he lived on larger and larger pillars until he moved to his last and highest one, which was about sixty feet tall! For thirty years he lived on these things—but of course, he couldn't quite manage to escape people either. For one thing, he had to eat. His food was sent up to him by means of a basket on a rope. Also, the strange sight of a man living on a pillar was bound to make people curious, so he got a lot of "tourists" coming out to stare up at him. Then, he was getting the same reputation for spiritual wisdom that other "unworldly" men did, and so Christians started

coming out to ask him for advice. His pillar was never so tall that his voice couldn't be heard from below, and in fact it made a pretty good pulpit, as he found when he began preaching to the crowds of people who came out to him. He also eventually let them put up a ladder so that visitors could come up and see him, and he would write letters and send them out to churches and even emperors. It is said that despite his strange choice of lifestyle, Simeon actually gave some good, sensible advice to people. And while you might think that having your dad live on top of a pillar all your life instead of in a house would not make you very inclined to "follow in his footsteps," that is, in fact, what Simeon's son did—and so did his grandson! How's that for a family tradition?

Simeon is an example of what became a more and more common practice in the days of the early church. Men began to live as individuals or in groups out in wilderness areas or deserts, away from the world. These people were eventually called "monks" from the word "mono" which means apart or alone. This is somewhat understandable, since there was so much persecution at that time. It was safer to be alone and away from things than to be in the world that hated you and sometimes sought to kill you! For some the temptations of the world were so great that they felt this was the only way to be what God wanted them to be. And in addition people truly did want to give up all they had to follow the Lord, to devote their entire life to doing God's will.

In the best situations, the early monks lived apart from the world, spending their day in the study of Scripture, and providing for their own needs rather than living off the community. Because they devoted themselves to the study of the Scripture, they learned a lot and became valuable teachers in the church. In that sense, the monks weren't a lot different from a full-time pastor, except that they usually didn't get married. Unfortunately, not being married became not just something a monk happened to be, but something he had to be.

This part of church history shows us how even though God wants us to be holy and "set apart from the world," this doesn't mean he wants us to run far away, or go up in the sky to get away from everyone (Matthew 5:14-16; Matthew 28:18-20; John 17:15). The only people we're strictly warned to avoid and stay away from are those who say they're Christians, and yet teach false doctrine, like those whom John and Polycarp[2] confronted) or who are living in open rebellious sin against God (1 Corinthians 5:9-11).

So, the world that God wants us to be set apart from is not the people of the world, it is the sinful, worldly distractions in our hearts (1 John 2:16). He wants us to run away from those, by praying against them, refusing to think about them and, sometimes, yes, leaving a certain place that makes them too close and too attractive to us. But as Anthony found, worldly thoughts can follow us to any physical place, even a bare, hard tomb; they must be fought against in the heart, right there in your home or your school or wherever, and not by trying to run away from them into the desert.

---

[2] See *Facing Lions* in Risktakers series Chapter 2.

On the other hand, there are positive things we can learn from the monks. First, we must have a heart of giving as many of the early monks had. It is easy to make excuses about Jesus not really meaning to sell all, but for some, that is exactly what He means! And all Christians must be open-handed about the things in this world, not allowing our hearts to be attached to stuff that will rot and perish very soon. The best thing about the early monks is that they were willing to give up anything and everything for Jesus. That's an attitude that is good and healthy for all Christians! All of us are to have our treasure in heaven, and disperse our goods to those in need here on earth.

The early monks also remind us how God uses imperfect people and systems to do His work. The monks and monasteries were the place where Scripture was copied and preserved, and where many of the good books about Scripture were written. Monasteries were also the base from which many faithful Christians, who were serious about serving God, lived and served, including people like Augustine![3] Bless God that we don't have to get everything right before He uses it to bring praise and honor to Jesus!

---

[3] Read more about Augustine and his mother in Chapter 7.

DEVOTIONAL THOUGHT

Think of the words "set apart." Simeon wished to set himself apart for God and that is why he went up on a pillar. But there are other ways to be set apart. Read these Bible verses:

> Acts 13:2 ESV: *While they were worshiping the Lord and fasting, the Holy Spirit said, "Set apart for me Barnabas and Saul for the work to which I have called them."*

> Galatians 1:15-16 NIV: *But when God, who set me apart from my mother's womb and called me by his grace, was pleased to reveal his Son in me so that I might preach him among the Gentiles, my immediate response was not to consult any human being.*

God set apart Barnabas and Saul for his work, and then Saul who was also called Paul wrote about how God set him apart from his mother's womb.

In the Sermon on the Mount, Jesus tells believers we are the salt of the earth and the light of the world. We are to be IN the world, seasoning and shining, but not OF the world, becoming polluted and corrupt. Are you willing to be "set apart" by being a shining light for God's glory? I hope so! It is the best and most fulfilling life you could ever live.

FACT FILE

Simeon was the son of a shepherd and was born at Sis, now the Turkish town of Kozan in Adana Province. Sis was in the Roman province of Cilicia, and after the separation of the Roman Empire in AD 395 it became part of the Eastern Roman Empire. Simeon lived for thirty-seven years on top of a pillar in Aleppo, Syria.

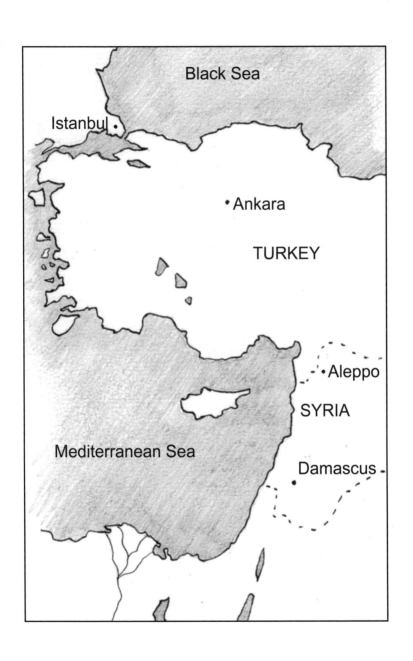

A MOTHER'S PRAYERS AND TEARS:

Monica (AD 331–387)

U sually when someone gets a place in church history books it is because of all the people they have reached with the gospel, or the books they have written, or sometimes even because they were such terrible enemies of God's people. Only a very few get mentioned simply because they were such wonderful, faithful parents. But that is exactly why the life of Monica is worthy of notice even to this day.

We know about Monica from the writings of her famous son Augustine. She was born in Northern Africa and raised by Christian parents, but they were not as careful with her soul as she was to be with her son's. They married her to a pagan husband, named Patricius. This man had a very bad temper, and it was common in those days for men to beat their wives. But Monica was an example of the Proverb that says "a soft answer turns away wrath" (Proverbs 15:1 NKJV), and her gentleness and meekness softened her husband's heart at least to the point that he was not violent toward her anymore. By her example and counsel, Monica was able to show many of her sharp-tongued friends how to control their natural anger and bitterness and instead to "win their husbands without words" (see 1 Peter 3:1-2 NIV). Even though Patricius was not violent toward her, he was not a faithful husband, either, and no doubt caused her much grief. However, after many years, her prayers and faithful witness to him bore fruit, and he, too, became a believer in the Lord Jesus, soon before he died.

Monica and Patricius had three children, but it was the brilliant, headstrong Augustine who caused her the most distress. She could not help but be pleased and proud of how well he did in school, but at the same time he showed that folly was very much "bound up in his heart." He confessed later that he lived for sports, and made it an idol, and he says he was even willing to cheat to win, and got very angry if the game didn't go his way!

Monica was faithful in teaching him right and wrong, but in their divided home, Augustine chose to follow his dad's bad example with women, and ignored his mother's pleas and warnings. In Augustine's opinion humility did not get one ahead in life. Self-control was no fun. Honesty was tiresome! Augustine says that everybody praised his dad for sacrificing for Augustine's education, but that Patricius didn't care about what was really important—Augustine's character and his soul's well being. While he was also growing in worldly knowledge, he was growing in pride, and learning how to be a smooth speaker. But God would use all of this for His kingdom in the future.

Augustine had some friends who liked to get into trouble. One time they all decided to sneak into a neighbor's yard and steal some pears from his tree. They weren't even very good pears, and Augustine knew he had much better ones at home; in fact, none of them really wanted the fruit, but they stole a 'huge load' of it anyway, and then tossed it to some pigs! Perhaps the neighbor had been going to pick them and sell them at the market to help buy food for the winter: Augustine didn't care. As he confessed later, he stole just to be stealing, just because he knew it was wrong! This is what our sinful nature does—it make us look at a thing that is ugly and disagreeable in itself, but just because it has a big FORBIDDEN sign in front of it we think it is great so we do it!

Augustine later talked about his behavior as a young man: "It was foul, and I loved it. I loved my own undoing." But he also says that being around other bad kids really made him much worse. He says that alone he never would have done the things he did! But when his friends talked about their sins, because he wanted to be cool and accepted, he even lied and said he'd done bad things that he hadn't done!

As Monica saw her beloved son walking further and further down the path of destruction despite all she could do or say, she decided to ask for help from the local pastor. Augustine wouldn't listen to her anymore, but maybe he would listen to a church leader? The pastor knew Augustine, and he knew that this would be like throwing pearls before swine, since the young man wasn't ready to listen to anybody right now. This response only made Monica feel helpless, because she could see how bad her son's condition was. But, when he saw her grief and her sobbing, he told Monica not to give up hope, but to keep praying and crying out to God, comforting her with these words: "It cannot be that the son of these tears should perish."

When Augustine was seventeen a rich friend of the family arranged for him to go away to Carthage, another city in North Africa, to continue his education. Being further from home, Augustine started believing more and more foolish things, until he eventually became a Manichean. The Manichean religion was a version of that old Gnostic heresy that the Apostle John so hated. This religion was started by a man name Mani, and he mixed a lot of the popular religions of the day into his, to make it very attractive to many people. It used a little of the language of Christianity to make itself sound good, but it taught that there was no Sovereign God, no accountability for sins and no need for salvation through the death of Christ. Instead, it said that there were two "gods," two powers, a good and a bad, equally powerful, and seen in man as the soul (good) and the body (bad). In order to become "good" a man had to identify with the soul part of himself, which if he tried hard enough he could certainly do.

One thing that Augustine must have liked about this religion is that it didn't condemn his sinful life. His ungodly attitude toward girls had long been a source of sadness to his mother, but now he stopped even pretending to have self-control, and moved in with a woman that he would live with for thirteen years but never marry. He even had a son, named Adeodatus. While he was in this false religion, or cult, Augustine could talk like a philosopher about great things, but he never had to confront his sinful heart.

Some books that Augustine read helped him see that there is more to this life than the sinful pleasures he sought. But at the same time, he said that he always felt like there was something missing in those books. The fact is that any book that didn't have the precious name of Jesus could not totally satisfy him.

Augustine became a teacher, and decided to move cross the sea from north Africa to Rome, Italy. He knew this would be heartbreaking to his mother. It was a move to promote his career, but she was sure he would only get farther from God when he was away from her and from the little Christian influence he had around home. He already believed in a foolish cult, what would he do now? Selfishly, Augustine didn't want to have to deal with a crying mother, so he decided to sneak off to Italy without even saying goodbye. But Monica found out he was leaving, and went to the coast to see him off, only to find that the boat had already gone. She felt like she had just lost her son forever! Again, feeling hopeless and brokenhearted over this prodigal son, Monica stood on the shore and prayed and wept for him. He had left the continent and her presence in pursuit of his sinful desires. Only God could change him, so she cried out to Him to transform her son's heart. God was guiding Augustine's steps without him knowing it at the time. He quickly found that Roman students weren't interested either in studying or in paying their school fees, which is bad news for any teacher. But a friend told him about a job in a nearby city, Milan. And who was the Bishop in Milan at that time—do you remember? Yes, it was the faithful emperor-confronting Ambrose! Augustine wrote later that he was "unknowingly led" to Ambrose, so that by him he might be "knowingly led" to God.

As we have heard, Augustine went to hear Ambrose preach, just because he was such a great speaker. When he actually met Ambrose, however, his feelings began to change. By the grace of God, the kindness and wisdom of this preacher began to work on Augustine's hardened heart. He decided to give up being a Manichee, although he wasn't yet a believer. He imagined his mother would be happy that he had changed beliefs to something a little closer to Christianity.

But Augustine being "not far from the kingdom" wasn't enough for Monica. Her husband Patricius had died, and she came to live near her son in Milan. As he put it, she was "following me over sea and land!" Although it was a dangerous journey, she was confident that the ship would not be wrecked, for, as she told the others on board, God had granted her a vision that she would reach land safely and see her son. When she finally arrived, Augustine was not slow to tell her of his changing beliefs. To his surprise, she was not excited at the news that he had left the cult. Instead, she told him calmly that before she departed this life, she would see Augustine a true believer. (Augustine notes that though she spoke so calmly to him, once she was alone she wept and wept, pleading with God for her son's salvation, just as she had always done.)

And Monica was not mistaken. God had begun a work in Augustine, and He was not going to pause until it was finished. God was chasing Augustine. If it wasn't Ambrose's faithful preaching and personal friendship, it was Christian biographies of people like the monk Anthony[1]. Augustine remembered reading about this man who forsook all to follow Christ, and he admired him so much. However, his sins and his worldly goods held his heart. There was a great struggle going on inside Augustine, and he was getting miserable with the fight!

Augustine knew that his mother's God was the true God, and that Christianity was the only way to obtain salvation—but he didn't want to give up his sins! He loved them too much, still. He would repent and turn to God one day—but not today: today he had other things he wanted to do. Maybe tomorrow! But tomorrow followed tomorrow, and still Augustine wrestled with his conscience and

[1] See *Facing Lions* in Risktakers series Chapter 7.

resisted. He says he actually prayed one time, "Make me pure, but not yet!"

Then, one day while he was sitting in his garden with a friend, he heard a child's voice coming from the house next door, singing "Take up and read. Take up and read." He remembered how Anthony had walked into a church and heard someone reading the passage:

> "Go, sell all that you have and give to the poor, and you will have treasure in heaven; and come, follow me" (Mark 10:21 ESV).

Augustine knew that these words were spoken to him by God. Surely, Augustine thought, this child's words are meant for me! He immediately took up Paul's letter to the Romans, which he and his friend had brought with them, and opening it, read the first thing his eye fell upon, which was this:

> "... not in revelry and drunkenness, not in lewdness and lust, not in strife and envy. But put on the Lord Jesus Christ, and make no provision for the flesh, to fulfill its lusts" (Romans 13:13-14 NKJV).

All his cherished sins, that he had been so reluctant to give up, suddenly were seen for what they were, and God was telling him to put them away and put on His Son! Augustine put down the book; he didn't need to read another word; he felt as if a bright, peaceful light had been shed over his heart. "Instantly," he wrote, "at the end of this sentence ... all the darkness of doubt vanished away."

His mother was there in the house, and he immediately came and told her what had happened. Can you picture good Monica's joy when he told her what God had done for him? All her prayers and tears had been abundantly rewarded, for not only was her son baptized by Ambrose, but her grandson Adeodatus as well, who was now a teenager and had believed in Christ too. (I expect, however, that

Monica didn't quite leave off crying, though now she no doubt cried tears of happiness.)

One day Monica and Augustine talked together about what heaven would be like, and how much better it was than life here on earth. Then, Monica told her son she was ready to go and be with the Lord. She said: "My son, as for myself, I now find no pleasure in this life. What I have still to do here and why I am here, I do not know. My hope in this world is already fulfilled. The one reason why I wanted to stay longer in this life was my desire to see you become a Christian before I die. My God has granted this in a way more than I had hoped. For I see you despising this world's success to become His servant. What have I to do here?"

Less than a week later, she became ill and died. Her last words were, "Nothing is distant from God, and there is no reason to fear that He may not recognize me at the end of the world and raise me up."

Augustine later spoke about the Christian life and testimony his mother left behind, "rising up and calling her blessed," showing that her works praise her in the gates, even to this day (Proverbs 31:28, 31). He said to the Lord:

"She was also a servant of your servants. Any of them who knew her found much to praise in her, held her in honor and loved her; for they felt your presence in her heart, witnessed by the fruits of her holy way of life. She had been the 'wife of one husband' (1 Timothy 5:9). She repaid the mutual debt to her parents; she had governed her house in a spirit of devotion (1 Timothy 5:4). She had a 'testimony to her good works' (1 Timothy 5:10). She had brought up her children, enduring travail as often as she saw them wandering away from you. Lastly, Lord … she exercised care for everybody as if they were all her own children. She served us as if she was a daughter to all of us."

Now that she had seen the "son of her tears" saved after thirty three years of praying for him, she left this earth to meet the Eternal Son, the One who will one day wipe away all the tears from the eyes of all His people forever.

DEVOTIONAL THOUGHT

Prayer is an important weapon in the hands of a believer, especially when there is a battle going on for the soul of an unbeliever.

If you have friends or family who do not trust in Jesus you can, like Monica did with Augustine, persist in praying for them.

The Bible tells us that we must pray without "ceasing." That means that we can and should pray any time of the day or night. There is nothing that can stop us from praying, and it ought to be a continual activity in our daily lives to call out to God from our hearts over the things that burden us.

When the Bible talks about the Armor of God it mentions that Christians need truth, the gospel, faith, salvation, and the Word of God as weapons to fight against the devil. It also says we need prayer:

> "And pray in the Spirit on all occasions with all kinds of prayers and requests. With this in mind, be alert and always keep on praying for all the saints" (Ephesians 6:18 NIV).

Yes, we need to pray for those who are unsaved, but as you can see in this Bible verse we need to pray for other Christians and the church – and everything else for that matter! The Lord is there to hear his children at all times and for all situations.

FACT FILE

Carthage is the city that Monica sent her son Augustine to in order to study. The city has existed for nearly 3,000 years. Built on a promontory with sea inlets to the north and south, all ships crossing the sea had to pass between Sicily and the coast of Tunisia, where Carthage was built, thus giving it great power and influence.

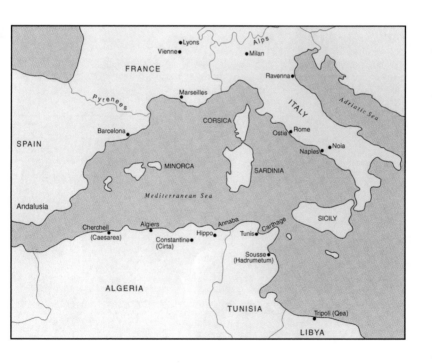

A REBEL RESCUED
Augustine (AD 354–430)

Augustine was again on a ship crossing the
Mediterranean Sea. But this was such a different
trip than the last one! The last time he was
sailing on this sea, he was leaving his mother Monica
on the shore of North Africa in tears, moving to Italy
in pursuit of more money and fame as a teacher of
rhetoric. He was also really hoping to get away from
any kind of Christian influence in his life. Basically,
he was trying to sail away from God! But you can't

run and hide from God when the Lord is determined to save you. His mother, and more importantly, the Lord Himself, caught up with Augustine in Italy and God saved him there under the preaching of Ambrose, as we've just seen in the life of Monica.

Now, in AD 387, Augustine was a middle-aged man who had recently and dramatically met Jesus Christ. He had gone from a selfish, lustful, false teacher who delighted in a weird religion to a humbled, obedient disciple of the Savior. Now, he was sailing with a whole different mission. Augustine had buried his mother in Italy, as she died the year after he was converted. God allowed her to see not only her son, but her sixteen-year-old grandson, Adeodatus, saved by grace before she died. Father and son were now returning to Augustine's homeland. Like several of the saints of the past who loved to read and study, he had plans for a quiet and peaceful life. He wanted to start a little community of monks where they would all work together to provide for themselves, and spend time meditating on and discussing Scripture. He had been inspired by the life of Anthony, which he read around the time of his conversion. So, he sold his family possessions when he got back, and he really didn't have much to speak of for the next forty years in terms of material goods. In fact, he didn't even need a will when he died, since all that he had already belonged to the monks he lived with.

Soon after coming to Christ, Augustine started writing books—LOTS of books! Sometimes, it is said that the toughest opponent is the one who used to be on your side. As you might expect, once Augustine became a Christian, the first errors he tackled were those of the Manicheans (which he had been before becoming a Christian). But though he now used his intelligence to point out the flaws in their doctrines so others could see them, God had taught him humility. Augustine did not speak harshly against them. In fact, he wrote that it was his duty to bear with them patiently, "as others bore with me in the day of my errors" when he was "blinded and maddened" by the same beliefs. Sympathy with them did not,

however, stop him from teaching against them so effectively that many people, including his friends, were rescued from their false teachings. That was just the beginning of many powerful writings to come from Augustine.

Sadly, a year after their return to Africa, Adeodatus became sick and died, leaving Augustine with no remaining family members. From that time on, he lived the simple lifestyle of a monk and never remarried. He hoped to live out the rest of his days in quietness and solitude.

Well, you probably know that we wouldn't be writing about him if that is all that happened! Augustine's time of living in retreat was pretty brief. He soon moved his group of friends to a city called Hippo, which was a larger city on the coast. Augustine wanted to move to this larger city to be able to reach more people for the monastery he had started, and he felt he would probably be left alone since there was already a leader of the church there. Well, he was quite wrong about that! Once his gifts were noticed and known, the church made him a priest and then a bishop. Goodbye to the quiet and peaceful life he had hoped for!

For the rest of his life, he was both a resident and overseer of the monastery, training pastors for the churches throughout North Africa. He was also bishop or overseer of several congregations, preaching in the churches and handling conflicts and problems among families and church members. And he was always writing something to try and help the church know God's truth better and respond to false teaching. The monastery carried on for hundreds of years. In its first generation, it brought about a great change in the African churches, through providing fresh, Biblical leadership to congregations across the region.

Augustine lived in a dangerous, exciting time. In the past, the church had been born and grown up in the shadow of the Roman Empire. That empire had continued for over 800 years. But in the last century, it had really started to crumble and fracture. It got weaker and more divided within, and that made it ripe for attack from outside. Little by little, more of the territory of the empire was being taken over or threatened by opposing armies.

As the armies came closer to the ancient capital of Rome, something else very important for the church was happening. The society and to some degree the church also was more and more corrupt. A devoted, well-spoken monk from Britain had moved down to the capital and was making an impact on the church in Italy, where Augustine had lived a few decades before. Pelagius was offended by the sin and ugliness of the scene. This was supposed to be the great Roman Empire?! This was the place where so many churches and Christians lived?! It was full of evil and wickedness, and deserving of God's judgment.

Pelagius began preaching against the sins of the city. He was a strong and passionate preacher, and he quickly gained a following. He rightly pointed out many of the bad habits and practices of the people, and he told them that they didn't have to live that way. They had the power in themselves to change if they only would do so. You might guess that a lot of people who didn't want to be confronted with their sins quickly began to hate this loud, arrogant little man! Others who wanted to see the city cleaned up, and people's morals changed for the better, saw him as a hero.

Now, we ought to mention that Pelagius was a self-disciplined man. He practiced what he preached in terms of keeping rules of behavior. He was respected for his morality and his self-denying habits as a monk.

But like so many with a fairly clean outward record, Pelagius didn't have much patience with people who talked about feeling enslaved to their sins. He had grown tired of hearing people say that they "couldn't" do this or that, as if they were in bondage to their sinful ways. He wouldn't take that as any kind of excuse for why someone wasn't doing exactly what God called them to do. So, he convinced himself and others that everyone really had it within them to do what God says. We just simply need to exercise our will power, resist what is evil, and do what is right.

For Pelagius, the main thing people needed to do was find the strength within themselves and determine to do the right thing. Sometimes, we talk of "pulling yourself up by your own bootstraps." That is the kind of thinking Pelagius had. And the thing was, for outward morality, it worked pretty well for him. He was a highly self-disciplined person. But there is a problem with people who have a lot of self-discipline – they can miss all the sin of their own hearts, and only look at their behavior (selectively). They can also be really hard on others, demanding that they just show more toughness and self-discipline. Most importantly, they seem to forget that pride and self-righteousness are also sins which God hates. In the case of Pelagius, he was pointing people to the WRONG place for the remedy to their problem of sin—themselves!

Some of the people began to respond to him about this teaching, and they actually brought up the name of Augustine. He heard from others that Augustine was teaching that there was no good in ourselves, and that we must cry out to God for help to change, because we are powerless to change ourselves. In fact, the bishop of Hippo had put it into a prayer to

God in this way: "Give me the grace to do as you command, and command me to do what you will! ... O holy God ... when your commands are obeyed, it is from you that we receive the power to obey them."

Maybe that sounds a little confusing, but it's a great prayer. Augustine was saying that he wanted to do whatever God commanded, but he asked the Lord to give him the power and help to do it. "Along with the command, Lord, please give the strength to DO what you command." In that way, whatever the Lord commanded Augustine would do. But without that grace and help from God, he was sure he would fail. He realized that every time he did something truly good and honoring to God, God's grace had already come before and given him the heart and the ability and the passion to do it. He couldn't take credit for his good works; they were the result of God's own work inside of him.

Now, Pelagius heard someone say this statement, and he immediately was upset with it. How could you ask the person commanding to give the power to do it?? The power to do it was to come from you, not the one doing the commanding! He fumed over what he saw as just excuse-making and weakness. In fact, Pelagius started teaching several things that weren't true from Scripture. The Bible teaches that we are born in sin (Psalm 51:5), but Pelagius said that we are all born pure and free, without sin. We don't have original sin, but just a bad example from Adam. Again, the Bible teaches that "all have sinned and fall short of the glory of God," but Pelagius taught that there were people who lived sinless lives and never disobeyed God (and we could be like that too!). The Bible says that salvation is only by God's grace, apart from our works. But Pelagius taught that our works help earn our salvation. What we do helps gain acceptance with God, not just what Christ has done on the cross. In fact, our works were the key emphasis of his teaching. According to Pelagius, that is what made us right with God or not.

So, the battle lines for one of the biggest conflicts in the history of the church were drawn. Pelagius was busy in Rome, spreading his teaching about the power of man to change himself and live a moral life as he ought. He believed the human will was free and capable of sinless perfection. "Grace" to him was just the common gift God gave everyone of free will and the good example of Jesus and other righteous and godly people. We all have that, so now it's up to us to do something about it! We need to get out there and live holy as we ought.

Meanwhile, Augustine had been spreading the message of the gospel of grace for two decades. He had seen in his own life that his supposedly strong "will" remained opposed to God and His Word until the Lord came in salvation and changed his heart by grace. He taught that there is not a single moment that any of us can do something good and right without the Lord being present to help us do it. He taught that our free will only ends up being used to pursue sin until the love of God is shed abroad in our hearts. He himself had tried to fight sin by his own will, but it was in vain until "the grace of God prevailed."

Augustine taught that God's grace is not just the natural gifts that all people have, but the supernatural blessing he gives to us apart from our works. Grace comes freely and unearned, or it is not grace in the first place! It comes beforehand, and moves us to respond differently than we could or would in our own power. And we never outgrow grace! We rely on and depend on God's grace all our lives. We will never reach a place where God owes us on the basis of our good record or our good name. Christ Jesus died not just as an example of self-sacrifice, but he died in our place – in the place of us sinners – to earn favor with God on our behalf, and to take our punishment away.

Now, you see that these two teachings were so very different from each other. They both knew there was a great gap between us and God. In a sense, Pelagius was trying to build a ladder up to heaven by works; Augustine believed that God built the ladder all the way down to us, and came down himself to rescue us.

While these two teachers were working in their own spheres, this conflict was only brewing; it wasn't in full force. What brought it to a head? Well, in God's amazing providence and wisdom, it was those wild barbarians from the North—the Visigoths.

We mentioned before that the Visigoths kept pushing and pushing, getting closer to the capital. Well, by the year AD 410, they had made it all the way to Rome. And when they got there, they tore the place apart! This army burned all kinds of buildings throughout the city and took anything shiny and pretty that they decided they liked. That included the emperor's daughter, who was kidnapped. (The general who led the Visigoths, Alaric, ended up marrying her later!) This was the first time the city had been threatened for nearly a millennium! You can imagine the shock and surprise when the citizens of Rome experienced rumors and sieges until the final onslaught came. The city they saw as a fortress that would never be overcome was now in the hands of people they viewed as inferior savages!

The invasion of the Visigoths drove thousands of people out of that region, and many sailed across to Africa. Pelagius was among them. And once he came to Africa and saw the influence of Augustine's teaching on the continent, he wanted to try and win people to his own view of self-help and human effort. That is where the conflict brewed into a full fledged battle.

For the first three hundred years or so of the church's life after the Apostles, the main battle had been about the PERSON of Jesus Christ. Christians died proclaiming Jesus is Lord, and the best church scholars wrote to defend the truth that Jesus is fully God and fully human, in One person, forever. Now, the main battle was becoming focused on the WORK of Christ. Augustine and Pelagius agreed about the Trinity and the deity and humanity of Jesus. But they differed greatly on the meaning and importance of what Jesus had come to do. They differed on his mission and therefore on the importance of grace and salvation.

I've already explained the differences between them, and I don't want to bore you with a lot of names of councils and cities and such. But you can just know that the church as a whole had many meetings and discussions in order to try and understand what God's grace is all about. Over time, Pelagius' teachings were condemned by more and more councils and church leaders. They began to realize that it was really the same teaching that the world has – be good, be a nice person, do your best … the power to change is within you. That teaching makes the very precious work of Christ on the cross seem meaningless. If all we need to do is try harder, and if our salvation is based on our works, why did Christ even die? If we can build a ladder up to God by our own righteousness, then the death of Christ was meaningless and in vain (Galatians 2:21). The gospel of grace is just that – good news (the "gospel") of God's undeserved, unearned favor! And Christians of the day realized and confessed that we are utterly sinful and needy in ourselves. They understood and declared that the grace of God alone is absolutely necessary for salvation. The work of Christ was not just to show us how to be holy, but to bear sin on our behalf. And having seen these things more clearly through the preaching of Augustine and others, they made decrees and confessions and agreements that this was truly the Scripture's message of salvation.

Augustine thought that there was really nothing as important as a true knowledge of the grace of God and the way of salvation. At the end of his life, he was still writing about grace and against the false teaching of Pelagius. Someone asked him why, and he said: "First and foremost because no subject gives me greater pleasure. For what ought to be more attractive to us sick men, than grace, grace by which we are healed; for us lazy men, than grace, grace by which we are stirred up; for us men longing to act, than grace, by which we are helped?"

The life of Augustine was long, and he wrote on many other topics as well. For the next thousand years, it is said, no one wrote with such insight and power as he had written. His works are still studied today and have many striking and helpful insights.

He was the most famous and most important church leader between the Apostles and the Reformation. That's saying a lot!! So, you should know that we have only scratched the surface of Augustine and touched on one major teaching that he emphasized in his ministry. He was a brilliant, varied, interesting, deep, intriguing, and many-sided character.

But all his brilliance didn't dampen his passion. Instead, his brilliance was the perfect complement to his fiery heart. It made him able to speak about the love of God and the joy of salvation with depth and clarity that few ever have since. His most famous book was his biography, *The Confessions*, which is written as a prayer to the Lord. He talks about how he tried so many things to give him peace and joy, but kept feeling troubled and empty inside. Nothing was satisfying him; nothing really could make him happy. He eventually figured out that God does that on purpose, in order to lead us to Himself. So, as he he prayed, he told his Saviour how he came to see that only God could satisfy the hunger of the soul. He said, "Our hearts are restless till they find their rest in You."

DEVOTIONAL THOUGHT

Ephesians 2:8-10 NKJV says:

> "For by grace you have been saved through faith,
> and that not of yourselves; it is the gift of God, not
> of works, lest anyone should boast. For we are His
> workmanship, created in Christ Jesus for good works,
> which God prepared beforehand that we should walk
> in them."

It is telling us that we are only saved by God's power not by our own efforts. In Augustine's life, we saw how important that truth was to him, and how he defended it and taught it to the church in his day.

Notice also, though, that the verse goes on to speak about how God has saved us in order to do good works that glorify him. He saves us by grace in order to showcase His grace in our lives by deeds of love and mercy. While Augustine was living as an unbeliever, God was preparing him for good works that he would do later in his life. The same is true for us who come to know the Lord. God has works prepared for us.

In his great mercy, He saves us by grace alone through faith in Christ. And having saved us, he begins to bear the fruit of good works in and through us by that same grace. What a marvelous privilege to be "God's workmanship," and to be a partaker of His amazing grace!

QUIZ: BASIL

1. Where was Basil born?

2. Who was Basil's special friend during his school days?

3. What was the name given to the emperor Julian?

4. What disease did Basil try to treat by starting a hospital?

5. What caused the emperor Valens to change his mind about Basil?

QUIZ: AMBROSE

1. Where was Ambrose born?

2. Where was Ambrose made bishop of?

3. Who came to hear Ambrose even though he didn't believe in Jesus Christ at that point?

4. What was the name of the emperor who came to Ambrose's church?

5. What insect often appears in pictures associated with Ambrose?

QUIZ: CHRYSOSTOM

1. What does the nickname "Chrysostom" mean?

2. What was the name of the emperor's wife who was against Chrysostom?

3. What happened in the city after Chrysostom was banished; it made the emperor's wife feel that God was judging them?

4. What were Chrysostom's last words?

5. What two structures was the city of Alexandria best known for in ancient times?

QUIZ: SIMEON STYLITES

1. What was the name of the strange group of people who lived on top of pillars?

2. How tall was Simeon's last and highest pillar?

3. How many years did Simeon spend on top of pillars?

4. Despite his lifestyle, what was Simeon good at?

5. Which members of his family followed him in this tradition?

QUIZ: MONICA

1. What did Monica's son Augustine steal one day with his friends?

2. Where did Monica send her son to study?

3. What did Monica do when she realised her unbelieving son had left her?

4. What did Augustine hear the child say in the garden?

5. How many years did Monica pray for her son before he was saved?

QUIZ: AUGUSTINE

1. What was the name of Augustine's son?

2. What was Augustine's religion before he became a Christian?

3. What was the name of the monk in Italy who spoke against Augustine's teaching?

4. Pelagius pointed people to the wrong place for the remedy for sin. Where was that?

5. Complete this quote: "Our _ _ _ _ _ _ are restless till they find their _ _ _ _ in You."

QUIZ: ANSWERS

Basil

1. Caesarea
2. Gregory Nazanzien
3. Julian the Apostate
4. Leprosy
5. Basil prayed for his son

Ambrose

1. Germany
2. Milan
3. Augustine
4. Theodosius
5. Bees

Chrysostom

1. Golden mouthed
2. Eudoxia
3. Earthquake
4. "Glory be to God for all things"
5. The lighthouse and the library

Simeon Stylites

1. Pillar Saints
2. 60 feet
3. Thirty years
4. Giving good, sensible advice
5. His son and grandson

Monica

1. Pears
2. Carthage
3. Prayed and wept
4. "Take up and read"
5. Thirty-three

Augustine

1. Adeodatus
2. Manichean
3. Pelagius
4. Themselves
5. "Our hearts are restless till they find their rest in You"

Risktakers Series

Adventure and Faith
by Linda Finlayson
ISBN 978-1-84550-491-5

Strength and Devotion
by Linda Finlayson
ISBN 978-1-84550-492-2

Fearless and Faithful
by Linda Finlayson
ISBN 978-1-84550-588-2

Danger and Dedication
by Linda Finlayson
ISBN 978-1-84550-587-5

Fighting Wolves
by J. R. Williamson and R.M. Freedman
ISBN 978-1-78191-154-9

Facing Lions
by J. R. Williamson and R.M. Freedman
ISBN 978-1-78191-153-2

CHRISTIAN FOCUS PUBLICATIONS

Christian Focus | Christian Heritage | CF4K | Mentor

Christian Focus Publications publishes books for adults and children under its four main imprints: Christian Focus, Christian Heritage, CF4K and Mentor. Our books reflect that God's word is reliable and Jesus is the way to know him, and live for ever with him.

Our children's publication list includes a Sunday school curriculum that covers pre-school to early teens; puzzle and activity books. We also publish personal and family devotional titles, biographies and inspirational stories that children will love.

If you are looking for quality Bible teaching for children then we have an excellent range of Bible story and age specific theological books. From pre-school to teenage fiction, we have it covered!

**Find us at our web page:
www.christianfocus.com**

CF4•K
Because you're never
too young to know Jesus